CARS ON MARS

Roving the Red Planet

Opportunity makes tracks on Mars.

Opportunity's false color panorama of Duck Bay in Victoria Crater

CARS ON MARS

Roving the Red Planet

Alexandra Siy

Charlesbridge

For my free spirits, Miela and Sasha—follow your dreams

First paperback edition 2011
Copyright © 2009 by Alexandra Siy
Photograph copyright © by various copyright holders

Published by Charlesbridge
85 Main Street
Watertown, MA 02472
(617) 926-0329
www.charlesbridge.com

Library of Congress Cataloging-in-Publication Data
Siy, Alexandra.
    Cars on Mars : roving the red planet / Alexandra Siy.
        p. cm.
    ISBN 978-1-57091-462-1 (reinforced for library use)
    ISBN 978-1-57091-463-8 (softcover)
    ISBN 978-1-60734-142-0 (ebook pdf)
1. Mars (Planet)—Exploration—Juvenile literature.
2. Roving vehicles (Astronautics)—Juvenile literature. I. Title.
QB641.S495 2009
919.9'2304—dc22   2008040751

Printed in China
(hc) 10 9 8 7 6 5 4 3 2
(sc) 10 9 8 7 6 5 4 3

Display type and text type set in ITC Goudy Sans and ITC Legacy Serif
Color separations by Chroma Graphics, Singapore
Printed in Nansha, Guangdong, China, by Everbest Printing Company, Ltd.
    through Four Colour Imports Ltd., Louisville, Kentucky
Production supervision by Brian G. Walker
Designed by Diane M. Earley

Acknowledgments
Cars on Mars has been a work in progress for several years, just like the rovers themselves. Many people have supported the project, both in spirit and by providing opportunities for insights and information. Thanks to Diane Bollen of Cornell University for her expert reading of the manuscript; to Jim Bell and Steve Squyres of Cornell University for their suggestions and for making the MER photographs accessible to the public; to Alastair Kusack and Jack Craft at Honeybee Robotics in New York City for a tour of their labs and close-up look at the RAT; to my editor Randi Rivers for her vision; to book designer Diane Earley for her imagination; to my son Sasha for zooming in on the planets with his telescope; to my father Bill Roberts for teaching me to play baseball and drive a stick shift; and to my husband Eric for sharing the journey.

Spirit's Husband Hill Summit Panorama

Get Directions

Start Address: Cape Canaveral, Florida, USA, North America, Earth

End Address: Gusev Crater and Meridiani Planum, Southern Hemisphere, Mars

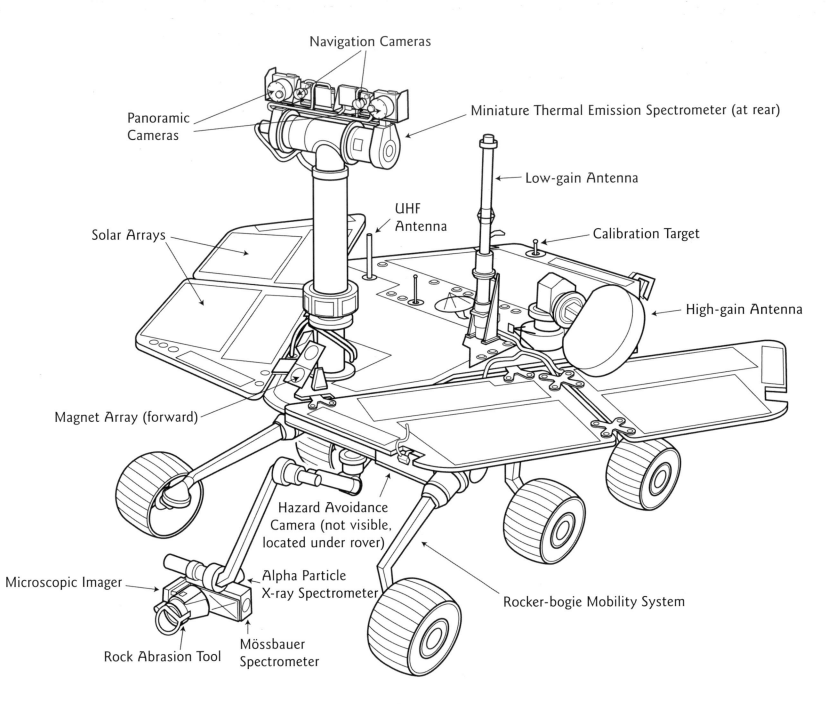

Navigation Cameras

Panoramic Cameras

Miniature Thermal Emission Spectrometer (at rear)

Low-gain Antenna

UHF Antenna

Solar Arrays

Calibration Target

High-gain Antenna

Magnet Array (forward)

Hazard Avoidance Camera (not visible, located under rover)

Microscopic Imager

Alpha Particle X-ray Spectrometer

Rocker-bogie Mobility System

Rock Abrasion Tool

Mössbauer Spectrometer

Mars Exploration Rover

Go 303,000,000 miles, then stop at the fourth rock from the sun

1

This composite photo shows the relative sizes of Earth and Mars. Galileo orbiter photographed Earth from about 1.3 million miles on December 11, 1990. Mars was photographed by Mars Global Surveyor in April 1999.

The summer of 2003 was the perfect time for traveling to Mars. Earth was closer to the Red Planet than it had been in sixty thousand years, and it wouldn't be as close again until the year 2287. Launching human explorers to Mars was still just a dream, but we could send the next best thing.

Why go to Mars? More like Earth than any other planet, Mars may have once been warm and wet. And if it was, might there have been life?

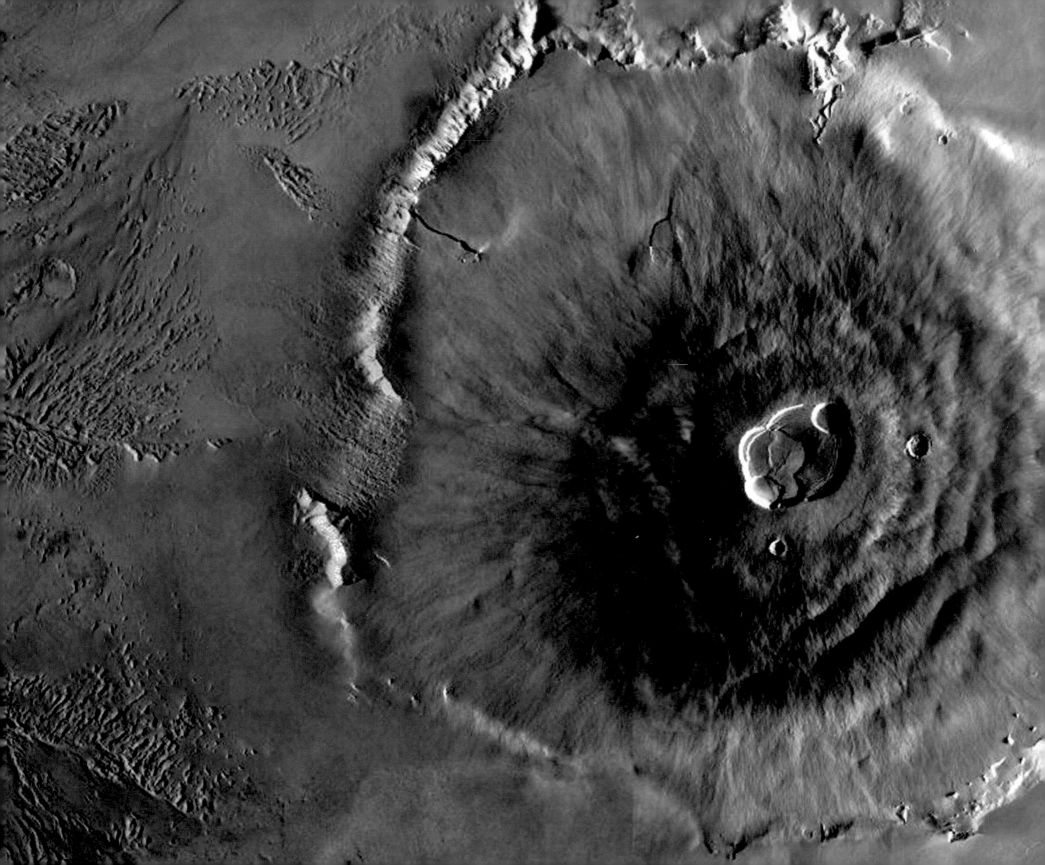

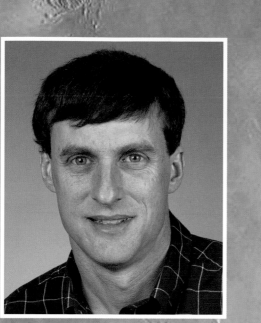

Dr. Steve Squyres is a professor of astronomy at Cornell University. He is also the principal investigator for NASA's Mars Exploration Rover mission.

Three times taller than Mount Everest, Olympus Mons is the largest volcano in the solar system—600 km (373 mi) in diameter, 24 km (15 mi) high. On June 22, 1978, *Viking I* took several images of the volcano, which were used to create this color mosaic photograph.

Follow the water

As a college student, Steve Squyres wondered about that very question after looking at photographs of Mars taken by the Viking orbiters. The year was 1977, and Steve suddenly realized that he wanted to go to Mars with a rock hammer in his hand to look for clues about Mars's geologic past. There could be no greater discovery, he thought, than to find out if life ever existed on Mars.

The Earth's surface is constantly changing from the action of wind, water, and shifting tectonic plates, which cause volcanic eruptions and earthquakes. Any evidence that might have shown how life first appeared on Earth is long gone. But the surface of Mars has remained unchanged for eons. Many rocks on Mars date back 4.5 billion years, to the beginning of the solar system. If life ever existed on Mars, there could be fossils of the very first life forms preserved in the planet's ancient rocks.

Determined to get a hammer on Mars, Steve and a team of engineers and scientists designed the "next best thing." Over the course of ten years, more than four thousand people worked together to build two robotic geologists for exploring Mars. Looking like cars rather than human scientists, the Mars rovers would study the history of water, climate, and geology on Mars, paving the way for human explorers. Their mission: Follow the Water.

Thank you for the *Spirit* and the *Opportunity*

The mission to send a pair of robotic geologists to Mars is called the Mars Exploration Rover (MER) mission and is part of NASA's Mars Exploration Program. The rovers were named by nine-year-old Sofi Collis, whose essay won the NASA Name the Rovers Contest, sponsored by NASA, the LEGO Company, and the Planetary Society.

"I used to live in the orphanage," wrote Sofi. "It was dark and cold and lonely. At night, I looked up at the sparkly sky and felt better. I dreamed I could fly there. In America, I can make all my dreams come true. Thank you for the *Spirit* and the *Opportunity*."

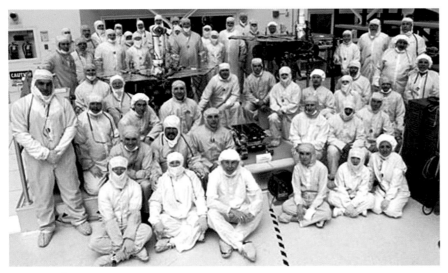

Rover team members in JPL's Spacecraft Assembly Facility wear protective suits to minimize the rovers' exposure to dirt and germs, which ensures that Mars won't be contaminated with life-forms from Earth. Pictured here is a fraction of the team that developed, assembled, tested, and launched the identical twin rovers *Spirit* (top left) and *Opportunity* (top right). *Sojourner*, the mini-rover on NASA's 1997 Mars Pathfinder mission, is shown in the middle of the team.

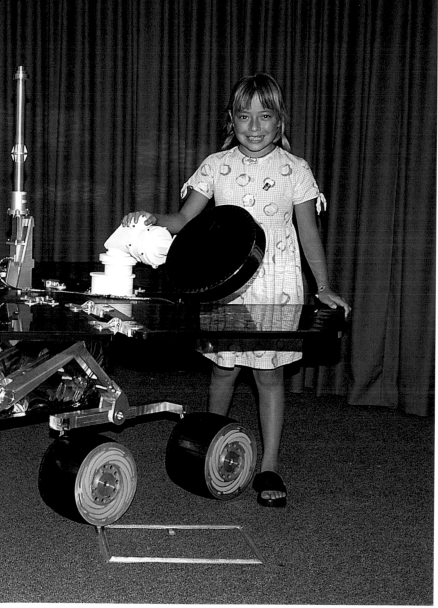

Sofi Collis poses with a model of the Mars Exploration Rover after winning the Name the Rovers Contest. Her essay was chosen from almost 10,000 entries. Sofi was born in Siberia and adopted by her American family when she was 2 years old.

Spirit and its lander were encased in the protective cone-shaped aeroshell at the top of this rocket. The disc-shaped cruise stage beneath the aeroshell was shed 15 minutes before *Spirit* entered Mars's atmosphere.

The rovers, which are about the size of golf carts, each weigh 175 kilograms (384 Earth pounds). Cruising speed is ten times slower than that of a wood turtle—averaging less than two feet per minute. Each car has six wheels and nine cameras, but no seats. The drivers sit in chairs—on Earth.

On the morning of June 10, 2003, *Spirit* was neatly folded into its protective lander. That afternoon a Delta II rocket launched *Spirit* into space from Cape Canaveral Air Force

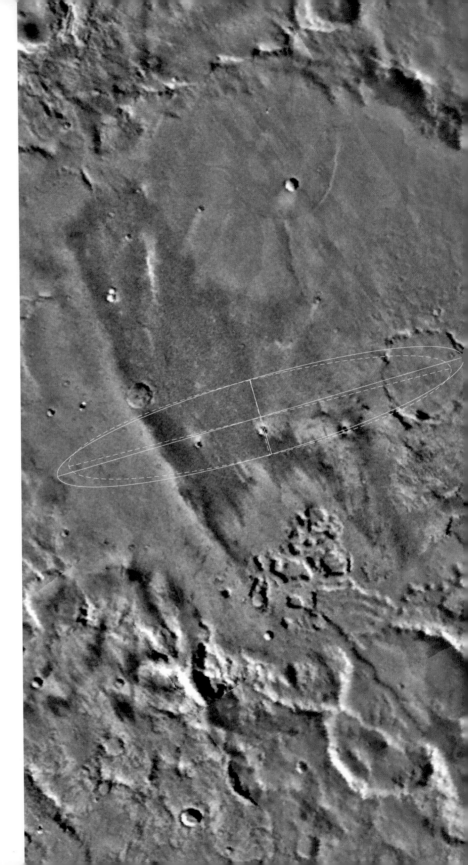

Station in Florida. Nearly a month later, on July 7, *Opportunity* took off into the night sky.

Where on Mars would *Spirit* and *Opportunity* land? At least one hundred scientists had argued the question for three years. They agreed that the two landing sites must be safe (not too rocky or windy), sunny (near the equator for maximum solar energy gain), and scientifically interesting (having good odds for important discoveries).

NASA chose Gusev, a massive crater the size of Connecticut, and Meridiani Planum, a wide, flat plain on the opposite side of the planet near the equator.

Look out below!

Almost seven months after takeoff, *Spirit* tilted, a maneuver designed to help it slip safely into Mars's atmosphere (picture a swan dive) rather than burn up from friction

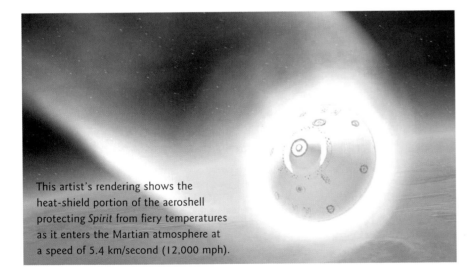

This artist's rendering shows the heat-shield portion of the aeroshell protecting *Spirit* from fiery temperatures as it enters the Martian atmosphere at a speed of 5.4 km/second (12,000 mph).

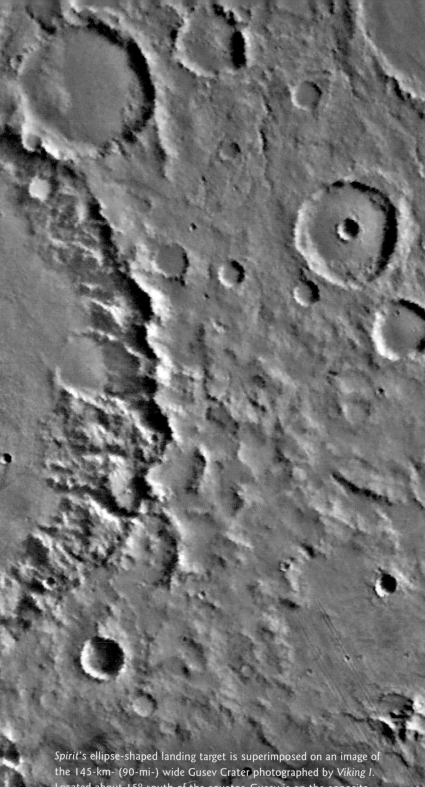

This artist's rendering shows the lander's parachute deployed and three retro-rockets firing as *Spirit* is suspended in its lander by a bridle 9 to 15 m (30 to 50 ft) above the Martian surface.

(think belly flop). Like an Olympic diver breaking through the water's surface, *Spirit* collided with the edge of Mars's atmosphere at 5.4 kilometers per second (12,000 miles per hour). For four minutes, friction slowed it down until the parachutes safely opened at 9 kilometers (30,000 feet). *Spirit* sailed toward Mars for two more minutes before, in a sudden explosion, the retro-rockets fired and the airbags inflated. Eight seconds later the spacecraft hit the dusty ground at 97 kilometers per hour (60 miles per hour). Looking like a bundle of beach balls, it bounced nearly 9 meters (28 feet) into the sky, then hurtled across the empty landscape, bouncing twenty-seven more times before coming to a quivering stop.

Spirit's ellipse-shaped landing target is superimposed on an image of the 145-km- (90-mi-) wide Gusev Crater photographed by *Viking I*. Located about 15° south of the equator, Gusev is on the opposite side of Mars from Meridiani Planum, *Opportunity*'s landing site.

This artist's rendering shows *Spirit* as it might have looked during its free-fall landing on Mars on January 3, 2004. Airbags designed to cushion the rover's crash landing inflate seconds before touchdown. Once the spacecraft has landed safely, the airbags deflate.

No one actually saw *Spirit* touch down in Gusev Crater. Instead, Steve and dozens of other scientists at NASA's Jet Propulsion Laboratory (JPL) in Pasadena, California, received information about its landing as codes displayed on their computer screens.

Spirit, phone home

Spirit's protective petals opened like a flower. Its solar panels caught the sunshine, and the mast popped up like a submarine periscope scanning the horizon.

The air on Mars is composed mainly of carbon dioxide and is too thin to hold much heat. On a summer day the ground temperature may soar to 35°Celsius (95°Fahrenheit) but plunge to −90°Celsius (−130°Fahrenheit) during the night. The rovers were built to withstand these temperature extremes, yet regardless of the temperature, they rely simply on sunshine to keep going. Driving, along with everything else, is powered by rechargeable batteries that store electricity generated by the sun.

Before driving off into the sunset, *Spirit* transmitted photographs of Mars back to Earth. Signals were beamed to one of the Mars satellites, which relayed the information to Earth's Deep Space Network (DSN)—one of three giant radio antennae located in Canberra, Australia; Goldstone, California; and Madrid, Spain.

Panoramic Cameras (Pancams) photographed the Mars landscape. Mounted high on the rover mast, the Pancams view Mars just as a human might while standing on its surface.

The radio antenna at Goldstone Deep Space Communications Complex is located in California's Mojave Desert. This DSN complex provides radio communications for NASA's interplanetary spacecraft as well as radio astronomy and radar observations of the solar system and the universe.

Scientists adjusted the colors in the pictures using the MarsDial, a calibration target mounted on the rear solar panel of the rover. They compared the colors in each photo with the chart on the MarsDial. This process is similar to fine-tuning the color on a television screen.

When scientists saw the rock-strewn, rust-colored ground and the clear salmon-pink sky at Gusev Crater on their computer screen, they were awed.

Sky in mirror

Bright shadow

This photo of the MarsDial, a color calibration target and sundial, was taken by *Spirit*'s Pancam. Mirrors on the sundial reflect the color of the Martian skies. The colored blocks in the corners of the sundial allow scientists to calibrate or determine the camera's sense of color, which is altered by Mars's dusty skies. Shadows cast on the sundial help scientists adjust the brightness of each image. The sundial also lets schoolchildren track time on Mars as part of NASA's Red Rover Goes to Mars Program.

Named "Mission Success," this is a section of *Spirit*'s first 360° panorama and was acquired during January 5 to 7, 2004. Panoramas are created from a minimum of 324 separate images that require at least six hours of photography. The images are merged together resulting in a mosaic with color seams. An approximate panorama color is determined using the MarsDial. The entire process of creating one panorama may take several weeks of work involving many scientists.

2 Roll forward, reach for rocks, then rove to hills and craters

Pasadena, we have a problem

A day on Mars is called a "sol" and is exactly twenty-four hours, thirty-nine minutes, and thirty-five seconds long. During *Spirit*'s first twelve sols of preparation, its electronic and scientific equipment was tested and activated, the surrounding soil was evaluated, and a plan was devised

This is an artist's concept of how *Spirit* looked after it drove off of its lander and into the dirt.

for *Spirit* to drive safely off the lander and onto the ground. Orders directing *Spirit* what to do and where to go were sent by radio signal from flight engineers on Earth.

It took another sol for *Spirit* to drive 3 meters (10 feet) to a chocolate-kiss-shaped rock. Although it was no bigger than a wizard's hat, the team named the rock Adirondack because it looked like Mount Marcy, the highest peak in New York's Adirondack Mountains. (New York is Steve's home state.)

Spirit's mechanical arm was outfitted with four scientific instruments for studying rocks and dirt. On sol eighteen, just after the arm reached out to Adirondack, *Spirit* shut down.

A team of software experts worked nonstop for three sols before diagnosing *Spirit*'s problem—a computer memory defect that caused *Spirit*'s operating system to crash and reboot in a nonstop loop. As the rover's batteries were drained to dangerously low levels, the software and systems teams continued their work day and night, like doctors trying to save a dying

Adirondack was chosen as *Spirit*'s first target because it had a flat, dust-free surface perfect for grinding with the Rock Abrasion Tool.

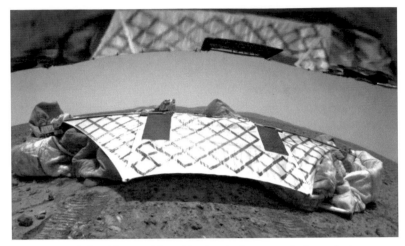

Spirit's view of the airbag-cushioned lander platform was photographed by its Hazard Avoidance Camera after the rover drove off the lander and into the dirt.

This image of *Spirit*'s robotic arm extended toward Adirondack was the first picture taken since the rover had shut down a week before. Photographed by the front Hazard Avoidance Camera, it shows how the Mössbauer Spectrometer (used to identify minerals) is placed against the rock.

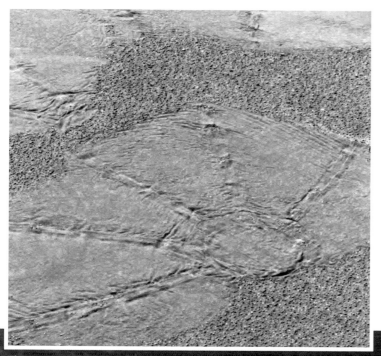

patient. When they discovered a way to interrupt the loop, more information was revealed, enabling them to fix the problem by devising a way to clear the flash memory (a type of memory that holds data even when the power is off) and access the random-access memory instead. Finally, after ten sols and a perilous brush with "death," *Spirit* could drive again.

Holy smokes!

Just as *Spirit* was getting back on its wheels, *Opportunity* touched down on the other side of Mars. It was a perfect hole-in-one landing inside a small crater, which was later named Eagle Crater, in Meridiani Planum.

The circular imprints made by *Opportunity*'s giant airbags during its landing on January 24, 2004, created a flower-like pattern the size of a basketball.

Opportunity took this photo on sol 1 after landing inside Eagle Crater at the Meridiani Planum landing site. The crater is about 20 m (65 ft) in diameter, and its rim is about 10 m (32 ft) from the rover.

The first pictures sent by *Opportunity* were out-of-focus black-and-white photos taken by the Hazard Avoidance Camera (Hazcam). The scientists at JPL silently watched the images appear on a big screen. Something in the pictures left them speechless. Then the Navigation Camera (Navcam) sent more pictures, confirming what everyone was thinking. . . .

All Steve could say was, "Holy smokes!" He forgot that the TV networks were broadcasting him live all over the world.

Opportunity had landed next to bedrock.

Bedrock is sedimentary, or layered, like a fancy cake. Sedimentary rock is scientifically tasty because it provides a geologic history—each layer is a look back into a different period of time. Bedrock on Earth formed over millions of years when layers of sand, soil, shells, and mud were deposited by wind, water, or ice and compressed to form solid stone. Was water involved in the formation of the bedrock on Mars?

Fancy cakes are indisputably delicious. On Mars, blueberries are arguably just as good: *Opportunity* was surrounded by tiny round rocks that were quickly named blueberries. The size of peppercorns or BBs (4 millimeters—0.16 inches—in diameter), the blueberries were actually dark red or gray in color, suggesting they contained hematite, an iron ore. On Earth, hematite often forms in liquid water. But it can also be made without water from the mineral magnetite, which is found in some kinds of volcanic lava.

Opportunity's mechanical arm couldn't pick a bucket of blueberries and send them home, but it could help scientists

The exposed rock outcrop in the wall of Eagle Crater was photographed by *Opportunity* on sol 17 (February 10, 2004).

figure out what they were. Geologists settled on three possibilities: they were little glass beads, like those formed from molten rock by Hawaiian volcanoes; they were tiny balls of compressed volcanic ash, like the ones that buried Pompeii; or they were small round rocks that form when minerals come out of liquid water to make solid spheres, like concretions found in many places on Earth. Steve and his team of scientists were thrilled, because *Opportunity*'s lucky landing would provide the evidence they needed to figure out what Mars was like on this spot a long, long time ago.

Opportunity's Microscopic Imager took this magnified picture of blueberries inside Eagle Crater on sol 13 (February 6, 2004).

If I had a hammer . . .

Instead of legs, the rovers have wheels. In place of eyes, they have cameras. On their movable arms they hold smart gadgets called spectrometers that measure the types and amounts of minerals in soil and rocks. And they carry the most important field tools of the geologist: a magnifying glass and a hammer. The Microscopic Imager is a photographic magnifying glass that takes close-up pictures. The Rock Abrasion Tool, or RAT, scrapes holes in rocks. Finally, Steve had a hammer on Mars!

There were many rocks inside Eagle Crater that looked interesting. To create simple points of reference and avoid confusion, rocks were given names, such as McKittrick, Stone Mountain, the Dells, and Last Chance—in honor of people or places on Earth, or for other descriptive connections. El Capitan, which was named after a sedimentary rock formation in Guadalupe Mountains National Park in Texas, was the first rock that *Opportunity* ground with its RAT. Scraping out a round cavity, the RAT ground through the soft rock until it hit a hard blueberry and stalled. Still, the RAT hole was deep enough to take a picture using the Microscopic Imager. Then the Alpha Particle X-ray Spectrometer (APXS) and the Mössbauer Spectrometer on the rover's arm analyzed El Capitan's mineral composition.

After several sols of gathering and analyzing data, geologists determined that El Capitan was made of a rare mineral called jarosite. Containing iron, sulfur, and trapped water, jarosite can form only in extremely acidic water.

Opportunity photographed its lander on sol 24 (February 17, 2004) as it prepared to drive out of Eagle Crater.

Opportunity's front Hazcam photographed its first RAT hole on McKittrick, a target rock on El Capitan. The depth of the hole was 4.4 mm (0.17 in), and it measured 45.5 mm (1.8 in) across.

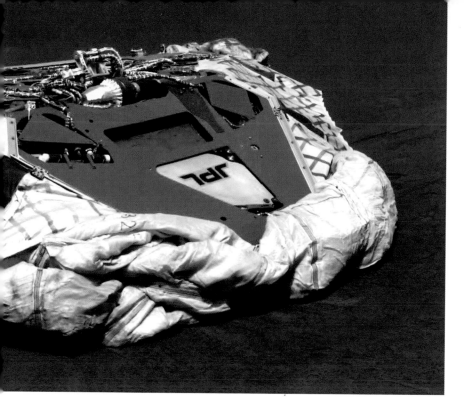

Berry Bowl in Eagle Crater shows the dust-free impression made by the RAT's brushes, and was later analyzed by the spectrometers.

Designed to study iron-rich rocks, the Mössbauer Spectrometer also analyzed the blueberries. Although its sensor head was small enough to fit in a human hand, its field of view was too big to focus on just one blueberry sticking out of a rock. A bunch of blueberries clustered closely together, like berries in the bottom of a cereal bowl, were needed in order for the Mössbauer to take an accurate measurement.

Wouldn't you know, the rover had previously taken a photograph that showed where a shallow hollow in a rock held a cluster of blueberries. *Opportunity* drove to this Berry Bowl and placed its Mössbauer on the rocks for twelve hours.

The results showed the strongest hematite signal ever seen on Mars (hematite was detected by the Mars Global Surveyor orbiter several years earlier), confirming that the blueberries were hematite-rich concretions (not glass beads or compressed volcanic ash)—in other words, they were iron-rich round rocks that formed in the presence of water. Already on sol 48 (March 13, 2004), *Opportunity* had found what it came looking for: proof that water once flowed on Mars!

Somewhere, over the rainbow

Looking for more evidence of water on Mars, *Opportunity* drove away from Eagle Crater at top speed, setting a record of 140 meters (459 feet) in one sol. Its destination: Endurance, a stadium-size crater named after British explorer Ernest Shackleton's famous ship, which was trapped by ice and crushed off Antarctica in 1915.

Meanwhile, by sol 65, *Spirit* had traveled 328 meters (1,076 feet) from its landing spot to Bonneville Crater, which was optimistically named after a prehistoric lake in Utah. Bonneville was beautiful but barren of bedrock. There were no yummy rock layers here, just solid stone formed from the fiery furnace of ancient volcanoes. *Spirit* rambled east toward the distant Columbia Hills. It was a bumpy and boring drive. If *Spirit* had had robotic children onboard, they would have complained, "Are we there yet?"

The MER mission was planned to last only ninety days, but *Spirit* and *Opportunity* kept on driving even after their three-month "warranty" had expired. When *Spirit*'s right front wheel motor malfunctioned, the drivers turned the rover around and switched into reverse. Driving backward for a

The Columbia Hills

Anderson Hill · Brown Hill · Chawla Hill · Clark Hill

The hills east of *Spirit*'s landing site are named after the Space Shuttle *Columbia* STS-107 crew, which was lost on February 1, 2003, during reentry into Earth's atmosphere. *Columbia* was commanded by Rick Husband and piloted by William McCool. The mission specialists were Michael Anderson, Kalpana Chawla, David Brown, and Laurel Clark; the payload specialist was Israeli astronaut Ilan Ramon. *Spirit* spent the first two years of its mission roving these hills.

Husband Hill   McCool Hill   Ramon Hill

while redistributed the motor oil and returned the wheel to normal operation.

It took ten weeks for *Spirit* to drive 2.6 kilometers (1.6 miles) from Bonneville to West Spur on the edge of the Columbia Hills, where it photographed a peculiar rock that geologists named Pot of Gold. Had *Spirit* come to the end of the rainbow?

Pot of Gold was small enough to hold in one hand, yet it raised some big questions. It had lumps sticking out of it and stripes running through it at odd angles—not like the neat layers found in sedimentary rock. The Mössbauer Spectrometer measurement showed that hematite was present, but that didn't prove water was involved (remember hematite sometimes forms without water).

Spirit's "Legacy" panorama was acquired about halfway between the rover's landing site and the rim of Bonneville Crater from sols 59 to 61 (March 3 to 5, 2004).

Almost two weeks after discovering Pot of Gold, *Spirit* was close enough to scrape out a RAT hole in its surface. During the grinding attempt, the rock moved and the RAT shut down. Still, the brushes cleaned enough of the rock's surface and the blades exposed enough of the interior for the APXS to take measurements. Sulfur, chlorine, and phosphorus were found—these three elements occurring together convinced scientists that Pot of Gold was once wet. After almost six months on Mars and nearly a month of work on Pot of Gold, Spirit had finally found a water-weathered rock.

As the Martian winter drew near, it was time to find a place to recharge. *Spirit* began the rugged climb up Husband Hill (the tallest in the Columbia Hills range)—with an unreliable right front wheel but a steadfast spirit.

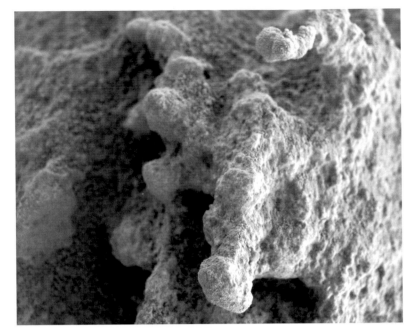

This is a magnified picture of Pot of Gold taken by *Spirit*'s Microscopic Imager on sol 163 (June 18, 2004). The area observed is 3 cm by 3 cm (1.2 in by 1.2 in).

You scream. I scream. We all scream for ice cream!

This false color image taken on sol 134 (June 9, 2004) by *Opportunity*'s Pancam makes it easier to see the layers of rock inside Endurance Crater. Each layer has slight color and texture differences and represents a separate chapter in Mars's history.

On the other side of Mars, *Opportunity* drove into Endurance Crater, where it found blueberry-filled bedrock all the way down to the sandy floor. Scientists spent months analyzing information collected from the crater by *Opportunity*, and they determined that there were three separate divisions of rock within a 7-meter- (23-foot-) thick stack. (Imagine scoops of vanilla, strawberry, and chocolate ice cream in a tall cone.)

The lowest, and therefore oldest, "scoop" was composed of dry, windblown sand dunes; the middle was an accumulation of windblown sheets of sand; and the top contained layers deposited by flowing water. The rocks in all three layers were

This panorama taken by *Opportunity* during sols 117 to 123 shows Endurance Crater and the surrounding plains of Meridiani Planum.

wet both before and after they were deposited by wind or water, suggesting that Mars went through a cycle of dry to wet conditions over time.

Experiments with imitation Mars rocks, which were made in the laboratory and then soaked in sulfuric acid (like battery acid), helped scientists conclude that highly acidic water (two thousand times more acidic than vinegar) had moved through the rock layers, causing changes such as the creation of blueberries.

This black-and-white mosaic is made up of 4 images from *Opportunity*'s Microscopic Imager and shows a "contact line" between two distinct layers of rock inside Endurance Crater. Contact lines represent periods of geologic time when significant environmental changes occurred. The observed area shown is 3 cm by 3 cm (1.2 in by 1.2 in).

The dunes on the floor of Endurance Crater were taken by *Opportunity* on sol 211 (August 27, 2004).

3 Watch your speed and enjoy the scenic overlooks

A picture is worth a thousand words

One year on Mars equals 687 Earth days, making each of its four seasons nearly twice as long as one season on Earth. *Spirit*'s first winter on Mars, which began in September 2004, was cold, with nighttime temperatures plunging to –110° Celsius (–166° Fahrenheit). *Spirit*'s power levels decreased as the sun sank lower in the winter sky and dust built up on the solar panels. Driving, photography, and scientific study were limited to less than two hours a day. The rest of the time, *Spirit* parked on a slope with its panels tilted toward the sun.

A simulated picture of *Spirit* was inserted in this photograph of Husband Hill.

Meanwhile at Meridiani, *Opportunity* snapped thousands of pictures of cliffs, clouds, stone, sand, shadows, and sunsets from inside Endurance Crater. Then, nearly one Earth year after crash landing on Mars, *Opportunity* visited and photographed the impact site of its heat shield, which was jettisoned prior to the rover's landing.

As spring slowly approached and solar power increased, *Spirit* resumed its drive higher into the Columbia Hills. Looking out across Gusev, *Spirit*'s Pancam snapped a series of photos

Three frames taken by *Spirit*'s Navcam show dust blowing across the plain inside Gusev Crater.

This mosaic of *Opportunity*'s heat shield impact site, which the rover visited in late December 2004, shows the main heat shield (left) with its metallic insulation layer turned inside out. The bright red circular patch (right) is the shallow crater made by the impact.

a few seconds apart. These "movies" showed dust devils, or slow-moving miniature twisters. Besides kicking up desert dust, the wind whisked dirt off *Spirit*'s solar panels, boosting its power.

Driving blind

Every move the rovers make is sequenced by drivers back on Earth. Using Pancam photos and maps, drivers look into the distance and choose the safest route. Then, as the rover drives forward, it snaps Navcam and Hazcam pictures, which help the drivers determine distances between points and avoid dangers, such as rocks and uneven terrain, along the way. The rovers' wheels are equipped to detect their own tilt and traction, which helps drivers prevent the Mars cars from slipping or tipping over. In February 2005, engineers updated the onboard driving software allowing the rovers to drive longer distances. In one weekend, *Opportunity* covered more ground than it had during the previous two weeks. Still, over the course of the year, *Opportunity*'s total driving distance was

This bright patch of soil, named Paso Robles, was churned up by *Spirit*'s wheels on sol 422 (March 11, 2005).

This is *Opportunity*'s photo of its one-day driving record of 177.5 m (582 ft) set on sol 383 (February 19, 2005) across Meridiani Planum.

less than two miles—just 3,014 meters (1.87 miles). *Spirit* was slowly making tracks, too—4,157 meters' (2.58 miles') worth.

While both rovers inched forward, they "looked" back by taking photos with their Hazcams—imagine rearview mirrors on film. But the Hazcams had a blind spot of sorts—they could "see" only in black-and-white. Once in a while, researchers used the Pancam to take color pictures of tire tracks. But these images weren't needed to make driving decisions, so they weren't immediately sent to Earth.

As *Spirit* struggled uphill, its wheels churned up ordinary-looking soil. Then a few sols later, scientists on Earth received a color Pancam image of the same soil, revealing its bright yellowish-white color. Steve was surprised. "My gosh," he said, "that soil looks very bright. We should at least take a taste!" The drivers stopped the car and made a U-turn.

Yellow is a sign of sulfur. *Spirit*'s spectrometers confirmed that the soil, later named Paso Robles, was mostly an iron sulfate salt and contained the highest salt concentration of

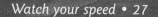

any rocks or soil found so far on Mars. "With this much salt around," Steve explained, "water had a hand here." On Earth, when ancient lakes evaporated, salt deposits were left behind—the same process occurred on Mars long ago.

That's meters per hour

There are no speed limits on Mars, only the limitations of the cars themselves. Early in 2005, *Opportunity* "sped" across the sandy desert, setting another driving record of 220 meters (721 feet) on sol 410. But on sol 446 (April 26, 2005), when it tried to drive over a knee-high ripple, its wheels spun for half a sol before the rover team realized its car was stuck in the sand.

How does a car get unstuck without a shovel, tow truck, or a person to push it? To find the answer, scientists on Earth

Opportunity was stuck here at Purgatory Dune, about 2 km (1.2 mi) south of Endurance Crater, for more than a month. It took this panoramic image, named "Rub al Khali" after an area of the Saudi Arabian desert, during sols 456 to 464 (May 6 to May 14, 2005) while there.

Inside the In-Situ Instrument Laboratory at NASA's Jet Propulsion Laboratory, Pasadena, California, rover engineers check how a test rover moves in simulated Mars sand.

mixed play sand, powdered clay, and fossilized diatoms (a soft, crumbly material used in swimming-pool filters) to make two tons of imitation Mars sand. Scientists stuck a test rover in their homemade dune and came up with a strategy: shift into reverse, drive, slip, and do it again and again, sol after sol, for more than a month until . . . ZOOM! *Opportunity* zipped backward out of its rut. From then on the Mars cars drove at slower, safer speeds.

Opportunity used its Navcam to capture this look back at the ripple it had been stuck in for five weeks.

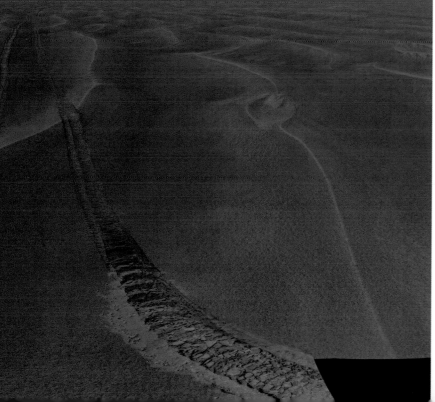

Water, water everywhere, but not a drop to drink

"Once upon a time, Gusev was a pretty violent place. Big explosive events were happening, and there was a lot of water around." Steve wasn't reading from a fairy tale but was describing *Spirit*'s discoveries to a meeting of the American Geophysical Union in New Orleans on May 24, 2005.

"In the last few weeks," Steve explained, "we have gone from a state of confusion about the geology of the Columbia Hills to having . . . a powerful working hypothesis for the history of these layers."

Spirit looked back to photograph this mosaic of a rock outcrop called Larry's Lookout on sol 442 (April 1, 2005).

Spirit's long climb up Husband Hill was paying off. When the Pancam sent home a photo from Larry's Lookout, layers of bedrock were revealed.

"That was the critical moment when it all began falling into place," Steve said. "Looking back downhill, you can see the layering, and it suddenly starts to makes sense."

During the Martian summer of 2005 (September on Earth), after a year of climbing, Spirit finally reached the top of Husband Hill. Rising 82 meters (269 feet) above the plains, Husband Hill would be, well, just a hill on Earth. But for Spirit, climbing Husband Hill was a monumental mountaineering achievement. "This climb was motivated by science," said Steve. "Every time Spirit has gained altitude, we've found different rock types. Also, we're doing what any field geologist would do in an area like this: climbing to a good vantage point for plotting a route."

While exploring the plateau and collecting clues, Spirit photographed a gorgeous glimpse into the geologic past: plains stretching far into the distance, where volcanic deposits covered all signs of an ancient lake bed. The hills exposed older layers that were raised and tilted (possibly by an impact from a huge meteorite), revealing what was hidden deep beneath Gusev Crater. By studying the sequence of these layers, scientists could piece together the events of the distant past.

Spirit photographed the summit of Husband Hill on Sol 614 (September 24, 2005).

A false color photo taken by *Spirit*'s Pancam shows a series of RAT holes.

4 "Park or Ride" for the next twelve months

Take me out to the ballgame . . .

During the twenty-one months since landing on Mars, *Opportunity* had driven a total of 5,737 meters (3.56 miles), while *Spirit* had traveled 4,827 meters (3 miles). As summer on Mars came to an end, it wasn't back to school for *Spirit*, but out to the ballgame. *Spirit* 's next destination lay downhill, to the south of Husband Hill. Dubbed Home Plate because of its distinctive shape as seen from space, this 1.8-meter- (6-foot-) high plateau was little more than 1 kilometer (one-half mile) away—a distance that took four months to cover.

This is *Spirit*'s view of the layered rock at Home Plate, taken while the rover was parked on the northwest edge of the rock. The area shown looks sloped because the rover was perched at an upward tilt when it took the image; however, the rocks along the rim of this vertical exposure are mostly level.

Spirit reached Home Plate in February 2006. It studied layers of coarse rock covered by finer rock grains—a pattern that could have been formed by blown-up rocks raining back to the ground. When *Spirit* discovered a spot where the layers were damaged, geologists speculated it was a bomb sag, made when a stone hit soft, hot rock (picture a golf ball landing in wet cement). Perhaps the explosion was from a meteor crash or a volcano. There was more to learn about Home Plate, but *Spirit* couldn't stay. Winter was on the way, and the solar panels were generating only half the electricity they did in the summer.

Something old, something new

Spirit drove slowly in reverse to a north-facing slope called Low Ridge Haven, where it could tilt its solar panels toward the low winter sun. This was not an easy task on only five wheels. On sol 779 (March 13, 2006), after spinning thirteen million times, *Spirit*'s right front wheel had stopped working for good.

Lasting eight times longer and driving eleven times farther than planned, the Mars cars were showing signs of wear and tear. The teeth on *Spirit*'s RAT were worn out, although the cleaning brushes still worked. Yet its performance had been brilliant: it had scraped fifteen rocks—five times more than it was designed to grind.

On the opposite side of Mars, *Opportunity* needed a mechanic. The motor in the shoulder of its robotic arm wasn't working. While the rover team made long-distance adjustments, *Opportunity* explored the ripples at Erebus Crater.

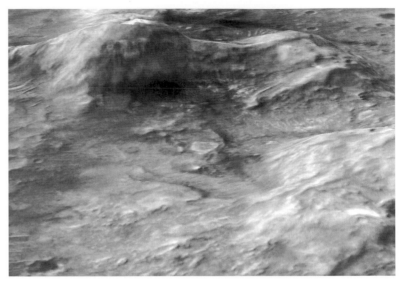

Using an image from Mars Global Surveyor's Mars Orbital Camera, scientists created this perspective view of part of the Columbia Hills range. Home Plate can be seen in the center.

The layers around the edge of Home Plate show a bomb sag, which is evidence of an explosion. The layers look straight and parallel except in the lower right, where they dip around a 4-cm- (1.5-in-) diameter rock that presumably fell into the soft rock.

An artist's concept of what the Mars Reconnaissance Orbiter (MRO) would look like above Mars.

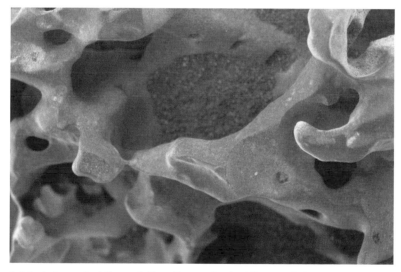

Spirit photographed the rock GongGong using its Microscopic Imager on sol 736 (January 28, 2006). Formed billions of years ago in a mass of lava, the rock captured tiny bubbles of gas. Then, for billions of years, it was weathered by sandstorms. Sand grains wore away the rock's surface until the delicate strands that enclosed the gas bubbles were broken, creating its spiny texture. The surface of GongGong records two of the most important and violent forces in Mars history—volcanoes and wind.

Up in the sky a new visitor had arrived from Earth. NASA's Mars Reconnaissance Orbiter (MRO) reached the Red Planet in March 2006 and would be ready to provide detailed mineral mapping, high-resolution images, and coordinated analysis of the scientific discoveries made by *Spirit* and *Opportunity* and transmit the data back to Earth by November.

Down to Earth

On Earth, scientists studied and analyzed the growing quantity of data and photographs provided by *Spirit* and *Opportunity*. They concluded that between 3.5 and 4 billion years ago, there was a lot of underground water at Meridiani Planum. Occasionally this highly acidic water bubbled up to form shallow ponds, puddles, and streams before evaporating and leaving behind salt deposits. Windblown dunes formed from the salt deposits and were preserved in layered rock.

Although Meridiani was dry most of the time and the water that sporadically spurted to the surface was caustic, scientists didn't rule out the possibility that life once existed there. After all, they reasoned, organisms on Earth called extremophiles thrive in equally brutal environments: acidic, salty, blistering, icy, airless, and highly pressurized. Could extremophiles have once lived, or even now exist, somewhere on Mars?

The only way to find out was to keep following the water. After two and a half years on Mars, the rovers were leading the way, slow and steady, yet full steam ahead.

A dream come true

Parked at Low Ridge Haven, *Spirit* hunkered down for the long winter but didn't hibernate. While studying soil, clouds, wind, and weather, *Spirit* photographed the magnificently detailed "McMurdo" Panorama.

Closer to the sun-drenched equator, *Opportunity* had enough power to drive year round. Finally, in late September 2006, after twenty-one months of travel, *Opportunity* reached the rim of Victoria, the massive crater 6 kilometers (4 miles) south of its landing site. Created by a meteor impact millions of years ago, Victoria was 800 meters (one-half mile) wide with rugged rock walls towering 70 meters (230 feet) above the sand-filled floor. Five times wider than Endurance, and forty times wider than Eagle, Victoria's 30- to 40-meter- (100- to 130-foot-) thick stack of layers (think maybe fifteen ice cream flavors instead of only three) offered a far deeper look into the past.

"This is a geologist's dream come true," said Steve as *Opportunity* pulled up to the edge of Victoria and peeked inside. "Those layers of rock, if we can get to them, will tell us new stories about the environmental conditions long ago. We especially want to learn whether the wet era that we found recorded in the rocks closer to the landing site extended farther back in time. The way to find that out is to go deeper, and Victoria may let us do that."

But *Opportunity* couldn't just drive into Victoria Crater like a sports car zipping into an underground parking garage. It took months of careful exploration to find the safest entrance.

The "McMurdo" panorama was taken by *Spirit* while parked for the winter on Low Ridge Haven. Scientists used information from this image to choose *Spirit*'s future explorations. Center are tracks and a trench dug by *Spirit*'s broken right front wheel, which exposed evidence of sulfur-rich salty minerals.

This mosaic was taken by *Opportunity*'s Pancam from sols 970 to 991 (October 16 to November 6, 2006). It shows the view of Victoria Crater from Cape Verde.

5 Avoid dead ends, drive through the dirt, and wait at ramp

Older but wiser

Can an old car learn new tricks? After nearly three years, scientists uploaded new software to the onboard computers that enabled *Spirit* and *Opportunity* to recognize and send new and interesting photos of clouds and dust devils and discard repetitive images. This capability saved researchers on Earth the time and trouble required to look through hundreds of images.

During sol 1,160 (April 29, 2007), *Opportunity* made these tracks while testing Field D-star, or go-and-touch technology, which allowed the rovers to plan long autonomous drives without help from drivers on Earth. *Opportunity* drove 15.8 m (52 ft) starting from the place near the center of the image where the tracks overlap—the other tracks in the distance were made by earlier drives nearer to the northern rim of the crater.

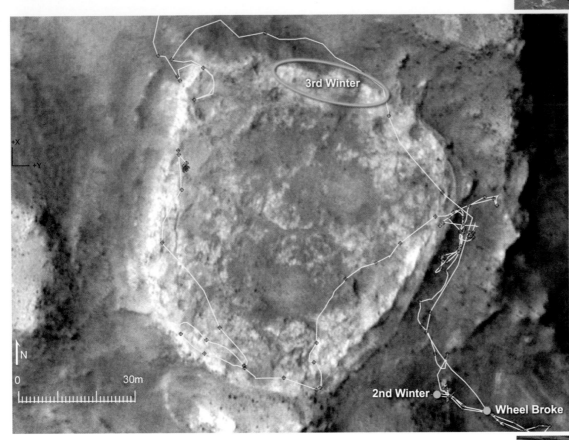

The yellow line on this map of Home Plate shows *Spirit*'s route from early February 2006 (north) to late November 2007 (western edge). Not shown is *Spirit*'s route to the area labeled "3rd Winter" where the rover waited out the Martian winter of 2008. The map covers an area about 160 m (525 ft) across from west to east.

New visual target tracking helped the rovers spot and keep track of rocks in the distance as they got closer. The Mars cars could also "think" several steps ahead while driving around a rock or ripple. Instead of backing away and trying different approaches over and over again, the smarter cars could find their way the first time. A dead end or even a maze couldn't stop or stump them. As independent thinkers, *Spirit* and

Spirit acquired this mosaic on sol 1,202, (May 21, 2007) while studying the area east of Home Plate in the Columbia Hills. The area of bright soil called Gertrude Weise was made by *Spirit*'s broken right front wheel.

Opportunity no longer had to wait for each and every order. Using the so-called go-and-touch technology, they could drive to a target, reach out their arms, and make contact, all on their own.

All-stars on Mars

On Earth, springtime marks the return to the baseball diamond; on Mars, it was time for *Spirit* to drive back to Home Plate. "It is one of the most interesting places we've found on Gusev Crater," said Steve. Scientists determined that the area near Home Plate was composed mostly of basalt (rock formed under extreme heat) and that the bomb sag was created by a volcanic explosion.

"When basalt erupts, it often does so as very fluid lava, rather than erupting explosively," Steve said. "One way for basaltic lava to cause an explosion is for it to come into contact with water. It's the pressure from the steam that causes it to go BOOM!"

On the way to Home Plate, *Spirit*'s dragging wheel dug a ditch in the dirt, exposing a bright patch. Named Gertrude Weise, in honor of the 1944 star left-handed first baseman in the All-American Girls Professional Baseball League, the soil was 90 percent pure silica—a discovery that made geologists gasp.

On Earth, silica is a plentiful mineral used to make glass. It's often produced in hot springs, where it easily dissolves from the surrounding rocks, like a sugar cube dropped into hot tea. When the water cools, the silica comes out of solution (think rock candy on a stick) and forms deposits. Silica is also deposited in fumaroles, which are cracks through which acidic steam spurts. On Mars, scientists concluded, silica was formed either in hot springs or in fumaroles.

Spirit also discovered high levels of the metal titanium at Gertrude Weise. On Earth, titanium levels are elevated in deposits made by fumaroles. Earth's hot springs and fumaroles teem with microorganisms, leading scientists to wonder if life could have evolved in a similar environment on Mars.

"This is a remarkable discovery," said Steve. "And the fact that we found something this new and different after nearly 1,200 days on Mars makes it even more remarkable. It makes you wonder what else is still out there."

Long ago, Mars was a lot more like Earth than it is now— a far warmer place where water flowed, filtered, flooded, seeped, streamed, steamed, splashed, spurted, swamped, surged, saturated, soaked, drenched, dribbled, dripped, doused, trickled, gushed, and poured.

But was there life?

On the edge

The Mars Reconnaissance Orbiter sent home a detailed image of Victoria. "If you were a geologist driving up to the edge of a crater in your Jeep, the first thing you would do would be to pick up the aerial photo you brought with you and use it to understand what you're seeing from ground level," said Steve. "That's exactly what we're doing here."

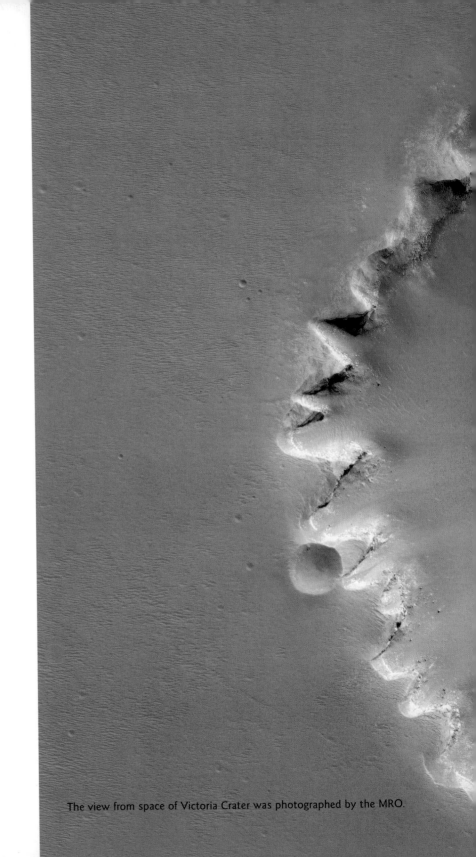

The view from space of Victoria Crater was photographed by the MRO.

While exploring Victoria's rim, *Opportunity* looked for stray rocks that were ejected from deep within the crater. Such rocks would be older than the exposed layers of sandstone. "We found one group of cobbles that were clearly more resistant to erosion than the sulfate blocks thrown out onto the rim," Steve said. "We checked the composition of one [and] our suspicion now is that [it] is a piece of a meteorite." Named Santa Catarina, it was the fifth meteorite the rovers had found so far.

In June 2007, *Opportunity* parked at Duck Bay, ready to drive down the gentle fifteen- to twenty-degree rock ramp— a slope that would allow the rover to get out as long as all six wheels kept working. "We don't want this to be a one-way trip," said Steve. "But if *Opportunity* becomes trapped, it will be worth the knowledge gained."

On the opposite side of the planet, *Spirit* accidentally ran over a patch of rubble while attempting to crush and expose the surface of a rock named Virginia Bell (after the power pitcher for the Springfield Sallies in the All-American Girls Pro Baseball League). The unintended "victim" was appropriately named Innocent Bystander and promptly analyzed. Scientists concluded that Innocent Bystander was probably formed directly in water by a hot spring or a fumarole— supporting previous discoveries made at Home Plate.

Like the unearthing, indeed the unmarsing, of the Paso Robles soils and Gertrude Weise, the encounter with Innocent Bystander demonstrated that scientific discoveries (on Mars as well as on Earth) are sometimes the result of errors, accidents, or surprise events.

Spirit's front Hazcam captured this wide-angle view of its robotic arm extended to a rock on the southern edge of Home Plate.

Shake off the dust, recharge at the rest area, and continue indefinitely

Out of the red

Then, "out of the red," a severe dust storm engulfed Mars, blocking 99 percent of the sun's light. Solar energy output plummeted to 128 watt-hours of electricity per day, equivalent to the amount of energy needed to light a 100-watt bulb for about an hour and a half.

(On a clear sol, the output averaged 700 watt-hours.)

On sol 1,224 (July 4, 2007), *Opportunity* photographed Victoria Crater during a dust storm from Cape Verde. In the foreground, *Opportunity*'s old (sol 959) tracks appear faded and dark under the new tracks made on sol 1,214.

A minimal amount of energy was essential to keep the rovers' electronics warm enough to survive. To save energy, *Opportunity* stopped all scientific study, and mission controllers suspended communication. Scientists wondered if they'd ever hear from the rover again. Near Home Plate, *Spirit* had barely enough power to keep in touch as it waited out the storm.

Three days later *Opportunity* phoned home. The little cars that were designed to last only three months had survived their biggest challenge in three and a half years.

In early September, as the dust settled, the rovers shifted back into gear. *Spirit* explored more rocks on Home Plate before tiptoeing down the northern edge where it tilted toward the sun and settled in once again for a long winter's nap.

Opportunity, the car that never quits, began its "Mars-shattering" drive into Victoria Crater—like a lone explorer from Earth walking ever so slowly, with wide eyes and an eager spirit, seeking an opportunity that might help answer the most tantalizing question of all: Are we alone in the universe?

Red rovers, red rovers, when will your road trip be over?

When this book went to press in late 2008, the rovers had been on Mars for almost five years. The mission had lasted nearly twenty times longer than planned, and the rovers had sent home more than 217,000 photographs while driving a combined total of about twelve miles. *Spirit* "slept" through most of the 2008 Martian winter, conserving as much energy as

This false color view from *Opportunity* on sol 1,433 (February 4, 2008) shows the lowest layer of three layers of bedrock that forms a bright band around the inside of Victoria Crater.

possible while waiting for the sun to rise higher in the sky and the wind to blow the dust off the solar panels. *Opportunity* climbed out of Victoria Crater and headed toward Endeavor Crater, located 12 kilometers (7 miles) away—a two-year journey. "We may not get there, but it is scientifically the right direction to go anyway," said Steve. "This crater is staggeringly large compared to anything we've seen before."

Measuring 22 kilometers (13.7 miles) across, Endeavor's rock layers are far deeper than Victoria's. "I would love to see that view from the rim," Steve said. On its way to Endeavor, *Opportunity* will travel through an area of cobbles speculated to have originated from deeper rock layers—providing the opportunity to examine much older rocks than seen in Victoria.

Although they found proof of past water on Mars (mission accomplished!), *Spirit* and *Opportunity* keep on keepin' on. No one knows when or where they will finally stop. But Steve and everyone else who is part of this far-out road trip hope that someday there will be tire tracks and footprints, side by side, on Mars.

This soil disturbed by *Spirit*'s wheel looks like a human footprint!

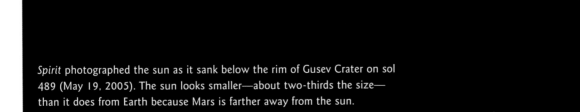

Spirit photographed the sun as it sank below the rim of Gusev Crater on sol 489 (May 19, 2005). The sun looks smaller—about two-thirds the size—than it does from Earth because Mars is farther away from the sun.

Message from Earth

I fell in love with Mars in the summer of 2003 while camping on an island in Lake Lila, a wilderness lake in New York's Adirondack Mountains. From the water's edge, Mars looked like a shimmering drop of vermilion-colored paint splashed in the night sky. It was closer to Earth than it had been in sixty thousand years, and space-ships from Earth were on the way there—I wanted to be a part of this interplanetary adventure. Although I couldn't hitch a ride, I could write a book!

During the four years I spent following the MER mission, I embarked on my own journey: a cross-continental road trip from New York to Alaska, where I lived and worked as a teacher. I learned much about "Alaska—the great land." Yet, I'm sure I discovered more about myself than anything else. Perhaps all journeys are the same   the places we seek to understand ultimately help us to know ourselves, our humanness. After all, it was not a picture of sand dunes in Endurance Crater or blueberries or a RAT hole that was chosen by people all over the world (including me) as their number-one favorite image from Mars. Instead, it was a photograph of a tiny sun setting above the Martian landscape—our sun.

In the summer of 2007, while the cars on Mars were braving a global dust storm, I returned to Lake Lila for the first time in four years. This time, Mars was not in view, but I knew it was there—and I wondered how much longer *Spirit* and *Opportunity* would last. As I scanned the zodiac, the band of constellations through which the planets travel, I realized it didn't matter. The adventure would never end, because we are on an infinite journey, an eternal quest, to understand ourselves, and our place in the universe.

Alexandra Siy, December 2008

Much more about Mars and the rovers

- *Spirit* and *Opportunity* will not last forever. Their end could be marked by power shortages as their solar panels accumulate dust and as Mars orbits farther from the sun. Unable to store enough heat energy and battery power to keep their temperature-sensitive equipment from freezing during the frigid nights, the rovers will shut down for good. Until then, *Spirit* and *Opportunity* drive on.

  To get the most up-to-date reports on the rovers, go to:
  Mars Exploration Rover Mission—Home at
  http://marsrovers.jpl.nasa.gov/home/index.html

- Mars is more like Earth than any other planet. Both Mars and Earth have four seasons, but the seasons on Mars are nearly twice as long as those on Earth. Mars has a radius of 3,397 kilometers (2,110 miles), compared with Earth's 6,378 kilometers (3,961 miles). Gravity on Mars is 38 percent of the gravity on Earth, meaning that a 100-pound kid on Earth would weigh only 38 pounds on Mars.

  For a complete comparison chart, go to:
  Solar System Exploration: Planets: Comparison Chart at
  http://solarsystem.nasa.gov/planets/compchart.cfm?Object 1=Mars

  To view the best images of these two planets, go to:
  Welcome to the Planets at
  http://pds.jpl.nasa.gov/planets/welcome/mars.htm

- Reaching a height of 24 kilometers (16 miles), Olympus Mons on Mars is the tallest volcano in our solar system and is three times the height of Mount Everest. Valles Marineris is Mars's biggest canyon; it measures 4,000 kilometers (2,500 miles) long.

For more fascinating facts about Mars, go to these websites:
Exploring Mars—Mars at a Glance at
http://www.exploringmars.com/science/ataglance.html

Star Date Online: Solar System Guide: Mars at
http://stardate.org/resources/ssguide/mars.html

- Mars has two small moons, Phobos and Diemos, that look a bit like baked potatoes.

  For more information about Mars's moons, go to:
  Mission to Mars's Fun Facts page at
  http://athena.cornell.edu/kids/tommy_tt_issue6.html

- The MarsDial, which fine-tunes the Pancams, also carries special messages from Earth, including drawings made by children. One message reads, "People launched this spacecraft from Earth in our year 2003. It arrived on Mars in 2004. We built its instruments to study the Martian environment and to look for signs of life. We used this post and these patterns to adjust our cameras and as a sundial to reckon the passage of time. The drawings and words represent the people of Earth. We sent this craft in peace to learn about Mars' past and about our future. To those who visit here, we wish a safe journey and the joy of discovery." The MarsDial even has its own motto: Two Worlds, One Sun.

  To learn how the MarsDial works, go to:
  Mission to Mars's MarsDial page at
  http://athena.cornell.edu/kids/sundial.html

- The rovers have taken more than 200,000 photographs of Mars.

  To view full-color images taken by the Pancams, go to:
  Pancam Images at
  http://pancam.astro.cornell.edu/pancam_instrument/ images.html

To look at all the photographs taken by *Spirit* and *Opportunity*, go to: *Mars Exploration Rover Mission: Multimedia: All Raw Images* at **http://marsrovers.jpl.nasa.gov/gallery/all**

- Humans have been exploring Mars since 1960. In the summer of 2008, the *Phoenix Mars Lander* touched down near Mars's north pole.

To find out more about this and future missions, check out the interactive timeline by logging onto:
Phoenix Mars Mission: From Earth to Mars: an Interactive Timeline at **http://phoenix.lpl.arizona.edu/timeline.php**

Visit the *Phoenix Mars Mission—Home* website at **http://phoenix.lpl.arizona.edu/**

To learn more about the past, present, and future of Mars exploration, go to:
Solar System Exploration: Missions: By Target: Mars: Past/Present/Future at
http://solarsystem.nasa.gov/missions/profile.cfm?Sort= Target&Target=Mars&Era=Past

http://solarsystem.nasa.gov/missions/profile.cfm?Sort= Target&Target=Mars&Era=Present

http://solarsystem.nasa.gov/missions/profile.cfm?Sort= Target&Target=Mars&Era=Future

- The rovers carry a memorial plate to honor the fallen Columbia Space shuttle astronauts. Information can be found at:

http://www.nasa.gov/missions/shuttle/f_marsplaque.html

- The Rock Abrasion Tool (RAT) on the Mars rovers was designed and operated by Honeybee Robotics, located in New York City. To honor and memorialize the people who lost their lives on September 11, 2001, aluminum from the World Trade Center was fashioned into cable shields for each rover's RAT.

To learn more about the RATs, go to:
RAT—Rock Abrasion Tool at
http://www.honeybeerobotics.com/rat.html

To learn more about all the scientific instruments carried by the rovers, go to:
Mission to Mars's Instrument page at
http://athena.cornell.edu/the_mission/instruments.html

- Although the information gathered by the rovers was taken from a tiny area of Mars, scientists used these discoveries to develop theories about the evolution of the entire planet. One of the biggest mysteries is how Mars could have been warm and watery yet lack limestone. Limestone is abundant on Earth and is formed by the carbon cycle. *Opportunity*'s discovery of jarosite inspired scientists to suppose that a sulfur cycle, similar to the carbon cycle on Earth, could have occurred on Mars.

To learn more about this theory, go to:
How Mars Could Have Been Warm and Wet but Limestone Free at
http://www.sciencedaily.com/releases/2007/12/ 071221130045.htm

- When will humans go to Mars? No one knows for sure, but some scientists predict humans will explore Mars sometime around the year 2050.

You can ask many of your questions about Mars and get an answer from Dr. C. at
http://marsdata1.jpl.nasa.gov/DrC/

Glossary

acid: A sour liquid that can dissolve metal.

Alpha Particle X-ray Spectrometer (APXS): An instrument mounted on the arm of each rover. The APXS measures concentrations of chemical elements in rock and soil samples.

basalt: A dark, dense rock formed from hardened lava; it is the most common type of volcanic rock.

bedrock: The solid rock found under loose soil or rocks.

bomb sag: A dent or hole created by a hard stone crashing into molten rock.

carbon: A nonmetallic chemical element found in all living things on Earth; it forms fossil fuels such as coal, and it occurs in its crystalline form as diamond and graphite.

carbon cycle: The constant flow of carbon from the Earth's atmosphere into plants during the process of photosynthesis, then back into the atmosphere from respiration (breathing) and decay (rotting) of plants and animals, as well as from the burning of wood, coal, gas, and other fossil fuels.

carbon dioxide: A colorless, odorless gas composed of one carbon and two oxygen atoms (CO_2). It's formed from burning carbon (wood, coal, and other fossil fuels) and during breathing (respiration) and decay (rotting) of plants and animals.

concretion: A small, globe-shaped stone formed from the buildup of minerals in sedimentary rock.

constellation: A group of stars that forms an outline of an animal, person, or thing in the night sky.

crater: A bowl-shaped hole made by an explosion, impact, or volcano.

Deep Space Network (DSN): NASA's three tracking stations located in California, Spain, and Australia. The DSN communicates with spacecraft flying outside of Earth's orbit.

Diemos: The smaller of the two moons of Mars; its name means "panic," and it was named after one of the horses that pulled the chariot of Ares, the Greek god of war.

dust devil: A mini tornado of dust that blows across the surface of Mars.

element: A chemical substance, such as carbon (C), hydrogen (H), or oxygen (O), that cannot be broken down into simpler parts, but can combine with other elements to form more complex substances, such as water (H_2O) or carbon dioxide (CO_2).

evolution: Any process of gradual change.

extremophiles: A microscopic organism that lives in a harsh environment under conditions such as extreme temperatures, intense acidity, or excessive chemical concentration.

false color: This refers to an image that shows a subject in colors that differ from those of a true color photograph. The effect is used to enhance subtle color differences in a scene and help scientists with mineral analysis.

fossil: The prehistoric remains or imprint of a plant or animal from a former geological period that has been preserved in rock.

friction: The resistance something meets when moving over or through something else.

fumaroles: A vent in or near a volcano that gives off water vapor.

geologist: A scientist who studies geology.

geology: The science of the history of the earth and its life usually through the study of rock and its physical changes over long periods of time.

Hazcam: The Hazard Avoidance Camera rides low on the front and rear of the rovers. It photographs low-resolution, black-and-white pictures to reveal obstacles and other dangers.

hematite: An iron-rich mineral that often forms in water.

iron: A soft, magnetic metal that easily rusts and occurs abundantly in certain ores and meteorites.

jarosite: A rare yellow or brown iron sulfate mineral that forms only in the presence of water.

lava: The molten rock that flows from a volcano or from a crack in the surface of a planet.

limestone: A rock formed mainly from calcium carbonate and deposited as a sediment by water.

MarsDial: The sundial mounted on each rover's rear solar panel. It's designed as a target for calibrating the correct colors in photographs taken by the Pancam.

Mars Reconnaissance Orbiter (MRO): This satellite, which reached Mars in 2006, studies changes in the water and the dust in Mars's atmosphere, looks for ancient seas and hot springs, analyzes surface minerals and layering, and relays information from the rovers back to Earth. The MRO has a camera capable of taking sharp pictures of things on Mars, even objects as small as a beach ball.

meteorite: A mass of rock or metal that has fallen to a planet from space.

microorganism: A tiny living thing, such as a bacterium or virus, that is too small to see without a microscope.

Microscopic Imager (MI): The camera located on each rover's arm. It takes close-up pictures.

Miniature Thermal Emission Spectrometer (Mini-TES): A spectrometer that is able to determine the composition of rock or soil from a distance.

Mössbauer Spectrometer: The spectrometer mounted on each rover's arm. It's able to identify minerals that contain iron.

Navcam: The Navigation Camera, which is mounted on each rover's mast. It shoots low-resolution, black-and-white photographs that help the rovers plot a route.

operating system: A set of programs for organizing the activities of a computer.

ore: A mineral that contains a precious or useful substance, such as a metal, that can be extracted or mined.

Pancam: The Panoramic Camera, which is located on each rover's mast. It takes high-resolution, color images.

Phobos: The larger moon of Mars; its name means "fear," and it is named after one of the two horses that pulled the chariot of Ares, the Greek god of war.

planet: A rocky or gaseous celestial body with an elliptical orbit around a star.

Rock Abrasion Tool (RAT): The grinding tool mounted on each rover's arm. It is used to brush and scrape rocks in order to expose their insides.

salt: A chemical compound formed by combining an acid (such as sulfuric acid) and a base (such as iron).

satellite: An artificial object that orbits a planet and is often used for gathering and transmitting information.

satellite dish: A bowl-shaped antenna that receives signals sent by a satellite.

sedimentary rock: Rock formed from particles that are deposited by wind, ice, or water and are made solid from pressure.

silica: A hard, crystallized mineral that is found in many rocks, soils, and sands.

sol: One day on Mars, which equals 24 hours, 39 minutes, and 35 seconds on Earth.

spectrometer: An instrument used to analyze the spectrum, or picture graph, of the radiation that's given off by rock or soil in order to measure physical properties and determine the rock's substance.

sulfur: A pale yellow, nonmetallic chemical element that occurs alone or is combined with other elements to form sulfides or sulfates (salt).

sulfuric acid: A highly corrosive, dense, oily acid containing sulfur.

tectonic plates: The huge structures that form a planet's rock crust.

volcano: A mountain formed above an opening in a planet's crust through which lava, gases, and steam spew.

watt-hour: The work done, such as lighting a bulb, by one watt (a unit of electrical power) in one hour.

zodiac: A word meaning "circle of animals" that refers to the band in the sky through which the sun, moon, and planets appear to move relative to Earth; there are twelve constellations of the zodiac.

Bibliography

Selected bibliography

Astronomy magazine's special collector's edition, Mars 2006.

Bell, Jim. *Postcards from Mars: The First Photographer on the Red Planet*. New York: Dutton, 2006.

Caitling, David C. "Mars: Twin Studies on Mars." *Nature* magazine, July 2005, 42. Scientific results of the MER mission.

Croswell, Ken. *Magnificent Mars*. New York: Free Press, 2003.

Golombek, M. P., R. E. Arvidson, J. F. Bell, III, P. R. Christensen, J. A. Crisp, L. S. Crumpler, B. L. Ehlmann, R. L. Fergason, J. A. Grant, R. Greeley, A. F. C. Haldemann, D. M. Kass, T. J. Parker, J. T. Schofield, S. W. Squyres, and R. W. Zurek. "Mars: Analysis Assessment of Mars Exploration Rover Landing Site Predictions." *Nature* magazine, July 2005, 44. Scientific results of the MER mission.

Kargel, Jeffery S. *Mars: A Warmer, Wetter Planet*. New York: Springer, 2004.

National Aeronautics and Space Administration, Jet Propulsion Laboratory, California Institute of Technology, "NASA Facts: Mars Exploration Rover," fact sheet, October 20, 2004. **http://marsrovers.nasa.gov/newsroom/**

National Aeronautics and Space Administration, "Mars Exploration Rover Launch," press kit, June 2003. **http://marsrovers.nasa.gov/newsroom/**

National Aeronautics and Space Administration, "NASA Mars Exploration Rover Landing," press kit, January 2004. **http://marsrovers.nasa.gov/newsroom/**

Ride, Sally, and Tom O'Shaughnessy. *The Mystery of Mars*. New York: Crown Books, 1999.

Sobel, Dava. *The Planets*. New York: Viking, 2005.

Squyres, Steve. *Roving Mars*. New York: Hyperion, 2005.

Webster, Guy. Jet Propulsion Laboratory, NASA Press Releases: 2003–2008. **http://marsrovers.nasa.gov/newsroom/**

Many of the websites listed in "Much more about Mars and the rovers" on pages 50–51, which are hosted by both NASA and Cornell University, were also used in researching this book.

Source notes

All quotes by Steve Squyres are directly from NASA's press releases. Webster, Guy. Jet Propulsion Laboratory, NASA Press Releases: 2003–2008. **http://marsrovers.nasa.gov/newsroom/**

Photo credits

Jacket

NASA/JPL, front; NASA/JPL-Caltech/Cornell, back

NASA/JPL/Cornell, i; NASA/JPL-Caltech/Cornell, ii–iii; NASA/JPL-Caltech/Cornell, iv–v; NASA/JPL, vi

Chapter 1

NASA/JPL, p. 1; NASA/JPL, pp. 2–3; Cornell, inset p. 3; NASA/JPL, p. 4; NASA, pp. 4–5; NASA/JPL/KSC, p. 5; NASA/JPL, p. 6; NASA/JPL, pp. 6–7; NASA/JPL, p. 7; NASA/JPL, p. 8; NASA/JPL, p. 9; NASA/JPL/Cornell, p. 10 (top); NASA/JPL/Cornell, p. 10 (bottom)

Chapter 2

NASA/JPL/Cornell/Maas Digital, p. 11; NASA/JPL, p. 12 (top); NASA/JPL/Cornell, p. 12 (bottom, left); NASA/JPL, p. 12 (bottom, right); NASA/JPL, p. 13 (top); NASA/JPL/Cornell, p. 13 (bottom); NASA/JPL/Cornell, pp. 14–15; D. Savransky and J. Bell (Cornell)/JPL/NASA, p. 15; NASA/JPL/Cornell, pp. 16–17; NASA/JPL, p. 16 (bottom); NASA/JPL/Cornell, p. 17 (bottom); NASA/JPL/Cornell, pp. 18–19 (top); NASA/JPL/Cornell, pp. 18–19 (bottom); NASA/JPL/Cornell/USGS, p. 20 (top); NASA/JPL/Cornell, pp. 20–21; NASA/JPL/Cornell, p. 21 (top); NASA/JPL/USGS, p. 22 (top); NASA/JPL/Cornell, p. 22 (bottom)

Chapter 3

NASA/JPL-Solar System Visualization Team, p. 23; NASA/JPL, p. 24 (top); NASA/JPL/Cornell, pp. 24–25; NASA/JPL, p. 25 (top, left); NASA/JPL, p. 25 (top, right); NASA/JPL/Cornell, pp. 26–27 (top); NASA/JPL, pp. 26–27 (bottom); NASA/JPL, pp. 28–29 (top); NASA/JPL/Cornell, pp. 28–29 (bottom); NASA/JPL, p. 29; NASA/JPL/Cornell, pp. 30–31 (top); NASA/JPL/Cornell, pp. 30–31 (bottom); D. Savransky and J. Bell (Cornell)/JPL/NASA, p. 32

Chapter 4

NASA/JPL-Caltech/USGS/Cornell, p. 33; NASA/JPL-Caltech/ MSSS/USGS, p. 34 (top); NASA/JPL/Cornell, p. 34 (bottom); NASA/JPL, p. 35 (top); NASA/JPL-Caltech/ Cornell/USGS, p. 35 (bottom); NASA/JPL/Cornell, pp. 36–37; NASA/JPL/Cornell, p. 38

Chapter 5

NASA/JPL-Caltech/Cornell, p. 39; NASA/JPL-Caltech/UA/Cornell/NM Museum of Natural History and Science, p. 40; NASA/JPL/Cornell, pp. 40–41; NASA/JPL/University of Arizona, pp. 42–43; NASA/JPL-Caltech, p. 44

Chapter 6

NASA/JPL/Cornell, p. 45; NASA/JPL/Cornell, pp. 46–47; NASA, p. 47

NASA/JPL/Texas A&M/Cornell, pp. 48–49; NASA/JPL/Cornell, p. 55; NASA/USGS, p. 58

This digital image of *Opportunity* was added to a photo showing the inside of Endurance Crater.

Index

A
Adirondack (rock), 12
  photo of, 12
airbags, 7, 8, 13
Alpha Particle X-ray Spectrometer
  (APXS), 16
American Geophysical Union, 30

B
basalt, 41
bedrock, 14, 18, 21, 31, 46
Berry Bowl, 17
  photo of, 17
blueberries (rocks), 14–15, 16–17,
  21, 22
  photo of, 15
Bonneville Crater, 18, 19
  photo of, 18–19

C
cameras
  Hazard Avoidance Camera (Hazcam),
    12, 14, 16, 26–27, 44
  Mars Global Surveyor Mars
    Orbital Camera, 34
  Navigation Camera (Navcam), 14,
    24, 26, 29
  Panoramic Camera (Pancam),
    9–10, 21, 24, 26, 27, 31, 32, 38
  Cape Canaveral Air Force Station,
    5–6
carbon dioxide, 9
chlorine, 20
Collis, Sofi, 4, 5
  photo of, 5
Columbia Hills, 18–20, 24, 30, 34, 40
  photo of, 18–19, 34
contact lines, 22
  photo of, 22

D
Deep Space Networks (DSN), 9
Delta II rocket, 5
  photo of, 5
diatoms, 29
Duck Bay, 44
dust devils, 26, 39
  photo of, 24–25
dust storm, 45–46
  photo of, 45

E
Eagle Crater, 13, 16, 17, 36
  photos of, 13, 14–15
Earth
  bedrock and, 14
  beginning of life on, 1, 3
  extremophiles on, 35
  hematite and, 14, 15
  salt and, 28
  silica and, 41–42
  size relative to Mars, photo, 1
  titanium and, 42
El Capitan (rock), 16
  photo of, 16
El Dorado (sand dunes), photo of,
  36–37
elements
  chlorine, 20
  iron, 16–17
  phosphorus, 20
  sulfur, 16, 20, 27, 36
  titanium, 42
Endeavor Crater, 47
Endurance Crater, 17, 21–22, 24, 36
  photos of, 20–21, 22
equipment. see also *Opportunity*
  rover; rovers; *Spirit* rover
  airbags, 7, 8, 13

cameras, 9–10, 12, 14, 16, 21, 24,
  26–27, 29, 31–32, 34, 38, 44
heat shields, 6, 24
  illustration of, 6
  photo of, 24–25
robotic arm, 12, 14, 16, 34, 41,
  44, 47
  photos of, 12, 44
rock abrasion tool (RAT), 12, 16,
  20, 34
solar panels, 9, 10, 23, 26, 34, 47
spectrometers, 12, 16–17, 19, 27
sundial, 10
extremophiles, 35

F
Field D-star, 39
fossils, 3
fumaroles, 42, 44

G
Galileo orbiter, 1
geology, study of, 3
Gertrude Weise (ditch), 41, 42, 44
  photo of, 40–41
go-and-touch technology, 39–41
Goldstone Deep Space Communications Complex, photo of, 9
GongGong (rock), 35
  photo of, 35
Gusev Crater, 6, 9, 10, 24
  evidence of water in, 30–31, 41
  photos of, 6–7, 24–25

H
Hazard Avoidance Camera
  (Hazcam), 12, 14, 16, 26–27, 44
heat shields, 6, 24
  illustration of, 6

photo of, 24–25
hematite, 14–15, 17, 19
Home Plate, 33–34, 41, 44, 46
  photos of, 33, 34, 36–37, 40
Husband Hill, 20, 23, 31, 33
  photos of, 18–19, 23, 30–31,
  36–37

I
Innocent Bystander (rock), 44
In-Situ Instrument Laboratory
  (NASA), photo of, 28–29
iron, 16–17
iron sulfate salt, 27

J
jarosite, 16
Jet Propulsion Laboratory, JPL,
  (NASA), 4, 9, 14
  photos of, 4, 28–29

L
Larry's Lookout (rocks), 31
  photo of, 30–31
"Legacy" panorama, photo of, 18–19
Low Ridge Haven, 34, 36, 37

M
Mars. see also individual names of
  geologic formations
  elements on, 20, 27, 42
  evidence of water on, 14–22, 28,
  30–31, 35, 41–42, 47
  length of year on, 23
  life on, 3, 35
  minerals on, 17, 19–20, 35, 41–42
  sand of, 28–29
  size relative to Earth, photo, 1
  sols, 11

Viking I took this photograph of Mars.